Wisdom

J.P. Vaswani

Compiled and Edited by
Dr. Prabha Sampath
and
Krishna Kumari

New Dawn

NEW DAWN
An imprint of Sterling Publishers (P) Ltd.
A-59 Okhla Industrial Area, Phase-II,
New Delhi-110020.
Tel: 26387070, 26386209, Fax: 91-11-26383788
E-mail: ghai@nde.vsnl.net.in www.sterlingpublishers.com

A Little Book Of Wisdom
©2003, Sterling Publishers Private Limited
ISBN 81 207 2587 5

Published by Sterling Publishers Pvt. Ltd., New Delhi-110020.
Lasertypeset by Vikas Compographics, New Delhi-110020.
Printed at Sai Early Learners Pvt. Ltd., New Delhi-110020.

The true teacher is a learner

all his life.

To live is to change.

Not to change is to be stagnant

and die!

To the weak, problems are stumbling blocks. To the brave they are stepping-stones.

Whatever you do, do it in the best way you can. It is your offering to the Lord.

It is alright to be disappointed. But we must never be bitter. Bitterness is a mark of emotional imbalance.

Which is the best city in the world? Simplicity.

The road is the same - uphill
or downhill.
Different people choose
differently!

Animals are happier than human beings because they are totally unaware of what is being spoken about them.

The worst thing that can happen to a man is that he has a hot head and a cold heart.

People are crazy to visit new places.

All that is needed is to develop new eyes.

From the point of view of physical strength, man may be weaker than many animals. But he is the only animal who can think.

There are three things that you cannot conceal - cough, itch and love.

The best of our friends are

our noble thoughts.

If you wish to be a citizen of the world, you must be courteous and kind to friends and strangers alike.

Many of us who need to mend put on masks instead.

How you die is very important. But much more important is how you live!

*The greatest fault is to think
that you are faultless.*

Life is too short to be spent in fault finding, holding grudges or keeping memory of wrongs done to us.

We all are seeking happiness:
A blessed few create it.

A man came to his Master and said: "Gurudeva, teach me."

And the Master said: "Go and unlearn what you have learnt – then come to me and I shall be able to teach you!"

Do you respect those who can be of no help to you whatsoever? Then indeed are you a true pilgrim on the path - a pilgrim of peace.

You are never too old to love,
but when you love, you suddenly
grow younger!

*L*et us feel grateful that many
of our dreams do not come true.
*I*f all our dreams came true,
many of us would not wish to
sleep at all.

The service we render to the less fortunate ones is the rent we pay for inhabiting the body.

*L*et the story of your life - like
any other story - be not
necessarily long, but it should be
thrilling.

Thanks to modern science, the earth has shrunk to a global village.

We all are kin. And yet we fight in the name of creed, race, nationality!

In this world there are things that need to be done! Why must I not be the first to do them!

We live in a world of flux.
Everything is moving to its
eternal drift.
Nothing stands still.

Living in this temporal world, let our gaze be fixed on eternity. That's where we are going to spend the rest of our life.

If the hearts of men are in turmoil, how can we have peace in the world?

Knowledge is good: and power is good. But without a sense of understanding, both are perverted into instruments of social chaos and destruction.

Why are we afraid of death?

Life is a series of changes and the greatest among them is what we call death. We cannot die. For life is undying.

Of what are we proud?
Wealth, learning, beauty.
But the wealth of the richest
tycoon, the learning of the most
learned, the beauty of the most
charming are little drops in the
totality of wealth, learning,
beauty!

*To the man who dares, there is
nothing difficult in the world.*

One rule of success is - always be on time and, if possible a little early.

Many a project has failed because the man who thinks it can't be done imposes his opinion on the man doing it.

Within every creature
dwelleth God.
So let us look at everyone with
wonder.
Let us treat everyone with
reverence.
And let us render to everyone
the service of love!
Speak sweetly, touch gently, look
lovingly and always long for a
darshan of the One who is in all!

True joy is of the heart. If the heart is happy, even a prison can become a palace!

The right way to live is to move forward and greet every experience - pleasant or painful - with a grateful heart.

Do not consider the faults of

others.

Do not criticise them.

Only love them - and keep on

loving them!

If marriage is a sacrament,
is not friendship equally sacred
and eternal?
Once a friend, always a friend!

A true friend is even he who will not hesitate to lay down his life for a friend.

Sympathy is a great healer. Keep on giving it to every sick person - also to every healthy one you meet!

Sympathy heals: sympathy strengthens: sympathy fills a person with new enthusiasm to do good to all.

*L*ove and joy are not
separate: they are but two sides of
the same coin.
*I*t is not a dollar or a rupee
coin. *I*t is the coin of selfless
service.

What is the most important thing for a man who would wish to tread the pilgrim's path? The first most important thing - and the second and the third are humility, humility, humility!

True humility does not consist in saying that you do not know anything but in admitting that you only know a little!

The life-breath of the life spiritual is humility! Lord! Grant me the grace of humility and make me as are Thy little ones!

The test of true greatness is – humility!

The best book is the book of the
heart.

Everyone has it: but how many
are there who can read it?

On the very first page of the
book are written the words:

"Take care of your thoughts!
As you think, so you become!"

In the dark of the dawn I saw seven poor people huddled together, lying peacefully on a heap of straw.

Towards the evening, two brothers met me. They lived in a huge, palatial house. They said to me: "The house is too small for the two of us: we must part!"

Never, never, never laugh at anyone - specially, when that person is hurting!

When you see a person's cap flying with the wind, do not laugh at the situation, but run and help him in retrieving his cap!

The more you grow in knowledge - true knowledge - the more you grow in love, devotion to the Lotus Feet of the Lord.

The Ultimate Reality is known by them who are humble of heart and are drenched in love.

If you would know, you must learn to love.

A great teacher said to his dear ones: "If you would know me, love me!"

Love, even when provoked, is never hurt. *Love* is patient and forgiving, loyal and trusting – and ever gives without any thought of receiving.

Think Little!
Feel Less!
Love more!

The aim of life is to realise that we are immortal spirits - not the bodies we wear.

To be meek and humble is to be invincible.

In a thousand water pots,
there is the one sky reflected.
When water pots break the sky
remains as before.

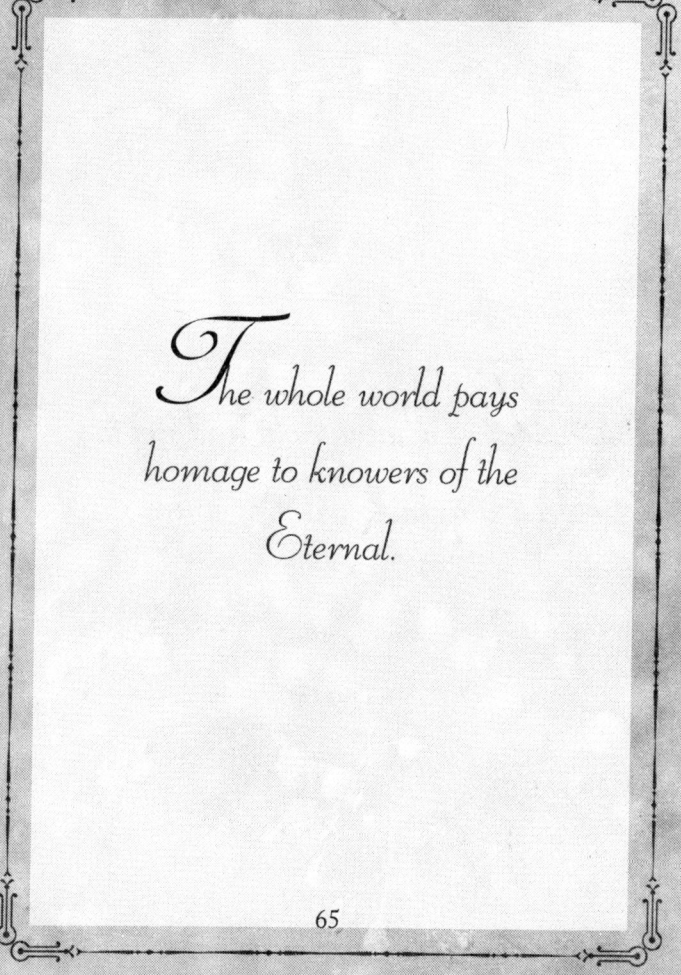

The whole world pays homage to knowers of the Eternal.

To see what is right and not to do it is to show want of courage.

Fear nothing! Fear only to do wrong!

Be ever patient and you
will win!

A man becomes what he
loves.

If he loves a stone, he becomes a
stone.

If he loves an object, he becomes
that object.

If he loves a person, he becomes
that person.

If he loves God, he will become
God.

Then why not love God?

Be a master, not a slave of

your senses.

To be able to come to God, you must first believe that He is!

The good persists. The evil
you do must find you out.

When love increases,

sensation decreases.

Speak little, serve more, and
love without ceasing!
Find fault with no one, smile all
the time and rejoice in whatever
the Will of God brings to you –
and your heart will be a singing
heart.
It will keep on singing.

Here on earth we are
judged by the number of people
who serve us.
There in the Kingdom of
God we will be judged by the
number of people we served.

Count your blessings and you will lack nothing!

*Misfortunes are blessings,
if we handle them well.
They are like knives which hurt
or help as we hold them, by the
blade or the handle.*

Life is a school and experience is our teacher. But the fees we have to pay are quite high!

*What is the noblest of deeds?
To forgive those who have
wronged us even before
forgiveness is asked – and to give
love to those who regard us as
their enemies.*

Make the people feel that they are better - and greater - than they think they are. And you will be helping them to bring out the best that is in them. And the best knows no limits.

Two things are essential to our happiness and peace of mind: love and work.

We must forget ourselves and love others - without any thought of return.

And we must do our work in love for God. The constant aspiration of the heart must be: "For Thy sake, O Lord! There is no other way to happiness and peace of mind.

We wish to help our friends

in a great way but such

opportunities come seldom.

Let us do little deeds of service

everyday.

And the good we do will never

pass away.

Nothing belongs to you
absolutely.
Everything is given to you for
use.
Therefore give all that you have
- and experience true delight.

A man is wealthy in the proportion in which his wants and desires decrease.

Character and success rarely go together. And character is always the better of the two.

You can't help growing in years: but you can always remain young in spirit. A woman of ninety said she looked forward to growing old. According to her, old age was always ten years ahead of her.

"*Faith*" and "*impossible*" - the two words can never go together.

Why wander here and there? The Truth is within thee!

"*I am my own ancestor!*"
said Karna in the
Mahabharata.
What family I was born in
and where, are matters of little
significance compared to
what I am.

We all cannot be great
scientists, artists, and teachers.
But we all can be a blessing to
those around us.

Success is getting what you want - and the wants keep on increasing.

To be truly happy you need to only count your blessings.

Every good thing comes as a gift from God. Of what can we be proud?

On the last day of my stay in London, I walked in Regent's Park and looked at the roses.

O, how beautiful they looked! Let me look at everything as though I was looking at it for the last time - and all around me the world will smile.

Do it - don't merely speak of doing it!

"Why must I not perform miracles to draw people closer to the Lotus Feet of the Lord?" I asked my Master.

And he answered: "To those that believe, no miracle is necessary. To those that believe not, no miracle is sufficient."

God provides food for the
birds: but they have to search for
it.

To be truly honest is to be beautiful.

What matters is not what happens to you, but how you react to what happens.

No external thing can hurt
you unless you give it the power
to hurt.

The wise man makes complicated things simple. The unwise man makes a simple thing complicated.

Let us do the little we can. If we don't do it because it's so little, we deprive the world of something.

Build your own temple and you will be happy, even if you are in prison.

If a man has not learnt to be patient, he has learnt very little.

If you want to achieve success, you must fix a goal - and everyday draw atleast one step closer to it.

He who is afraid to ask

will learn nothing.

Stop complaining: Start thanking.

*Everything in nature
proclaims God.
What about you, O man?*

Blessed are those who turn

away from impurity.

Yet they need to take one more

step.

They must give up all

consciousness of purity.

For the heart must be cleansed

of every stain of vanity before it

can be offered to the Lord.

The best ornament is
humility.
The richest wealth is wisdom.
The strongest weapon is
patience.
The best security is faith.
The most effective tonic is
laughter.

Put God before everything else and all things will fit in like a jig-saw puzzle - and life will be rich in the music of harmony and peace.

$\mathcal{T}$ime is running short.

The goal is still afar.

If you wish to reach it, you

must run!

Dada J.P. Vaswani needs no introduction to readers of inspirational literature. He is regarded as one of the leading spiritual luminaries of India, a practical philosopher and man of God whose grace has reached and influenced thousands of people all over the world.

A gifted writer and brilliant orator, Dada J.P. Vaswani has been the recipient of several honours, including the prestigious U Thant Peace Award. He has written over 80 books which have been translated into several Indian and foreign languages.